How To Use Systematic Attention and Approval

SECOND EDITION

R. Vance Hall
and
Marilyn L. Hall

How To Manage Behavior Series

R. Vance Hall
and
Marilyn L. Hall
Series Editors

pro·ec
An International Publisher
8700 Shoal Creek Boulevard
Austin, Texas 78757-6897
800/897-3202 Fax·800/397-7633
Order online at http://www.proedinc.com

8700 Shoal Creek Boulevard
Austin, Texas 78757-6897
800/897-3202 Fax 800/397-7633
Order online at http://www.proedinc.com

Library of Congress Cataloging-in-Publication Data

Hall, R. Vance (Robert Vance), 1928–
    How to use systematic attention and approval / R. Vance Hall,
Marilyn L. Hall.—2nd ed.
        p.   cm.—(How to manage behavior series)
    Includes bibliographical references and index.
    ISBN 0-89079-767-6 (alk. paper)
    1. Behavior modification.   2. Vigilance (Psychology)
  3. Reinforcement (psychology)   I. Hall, Marilyn C.   II. Title.
  III. Series.
LB1060.2.H355   1998
371.39'3—dc21
                                                    97-43040
                                                      CIP

This book is designed in Palatino and Frutiger.

Printed in the United States of America
    6   7   8   9   10   11   12   13   14   17   16   15   14   13   12

Contents

Preface to Series

The first edition of the *How To Manage Behavior Series* was launched some 15 years ago in response to a perceived need for teaching aids that could be used by therapists and trainers. The widespread demand for the series has demonstrated the need by therapists and trainers for nontechnical materials for training and treatment aids for parents, teachers, and students. Publication of this revised series includes many updated titles of the original series. In addition, several new titles have been added, largely in response to therapists and trainers who have used the series. A few titles of the original series that proved to be in less demand have been replaced. We hope the new titles will increase the usefulness of the series.

The editors are indebted to Steven Mathews, Vice President of PRO-ED, who was instrumental in the production of the revised series, as was Robert K. Hoyt, Jr. of H & H Enterprises in producing the original version.

These books are designed to teach practitioners, including parents, specific behavioral procedures to use in managing the behaviors of children, students, and other persons whose behavior may be creating disruption or interference at home, at school, or on the job. The books are nontechnical, step-by-step instructional manuals that define the procedure, provide numerous examples, and allow the reader to make oral or written responses.

The exercises in these books are designed to be used under the direction of someone (usually a professional) with a background in the behavioral principles and procedures on which the techniques are based.

The booklets in the series are similar in format but are flexible enough to be adapted to a number of different teaching situations and training environments.

As always, we invite your comments, suggestions, and questions. We are always happy to hear of your successes in changing your own behaviors and the behaviors of other persons to make your lives more pleasant, productive, and purposeful.

R. Vance Hall &
Marilyn L. Hall,
Series Editors

How To Manage Behavior Series

How To Maintain Behavior

How To Motivate Others Through Feedback

How To Negotiate a Behavioral Contract

How To Select Reinforcers

How To Teach Social Skills

How To Teach Through Modeling and Imitation

How To Use Group Contingencies

How To Use Planned Ignoring

How To Use Prompts To Initiate Behavior

How To Use Response Cost

How To Use Systematic Attention and Approval

How To Use Time-Out

Introduction

Social reinforcement has long been recognized as one of the most, if not the most, powerful way to motivate others. Dale Carnegie and Norman Vincent Peale were famous advocates of using social reinforcement or systematic attention and approval to win friends and influence people.

Good salespersons, effective leaders, and people who are popular with their peers are invariably persons who are skilled at giving social reinforcement. Some appear to develop and use these skills naturally and intuitively. Not everybody is so lucky, however. Nevertheless, behavioral research has shown that social reinforcement is a powerful force that almost anyone can use if they learn to apply systematic attention and approval to bring about behavior change. This book presents a program designed to help therapists and trainers to become more skillful in using this powerful and effective motivational tool.

How To Be a Better Motivator

Almost everyone likes to be liked. Most people would also like to be better at motivating those with whom they live and work so they will do their best. Parents like to find ways to get their children to behave well so they will have better family relationships. Teachers and employers want to motivate their students and workers to better performance while being enthusiastic about their work.

This book will help you learn to understand and use your attention and approval more effectively to bring about desirable behavior in those with whom you live and work. At the same time, following the techniques described will cause them to respond more positively to the more positive aspects of your own personality.

The techniques presented in this book are based on years of fundamental and functional research conducted in real-life settings. Much of that research was conducted by parents, teachers, employers, and others whose chief interests were in results rather than theory. This book is thus a device to provide information and to give exercises to help you use your attention and

R. Vance Hall, PhD, is Senior Scientist Emeritus of The Bureau of Child Research and Professor Emeritus of Human Development and Family Life and Special Education at the University of Kansas. He was a pioneer in carrying out behavioral research in classrooms and in homes. Marilyn L. Hall, EdD, taught and carried out research in regular and special public school classrooms. While at the University of Kansas, she developed programs for training parents to use systematic behavior change procedures and was a successful behavior therapist specializing in child management and marriage relationships.

approval to motivate others to improve themselves. It will require some effort from you, but that investment of effort will pay great dividends.

Only in recent years have psychologists recognized how powerful adult attention can be. Those who learn to use it effectively have a distinct advantage in their relationships with their children, their students, employees, relatives, and friends.

The exercises in this book can be used alone, but are better used under the direction of someone (usually a professional) who has a background in behavior management and experience in the application of systematic attention and approval. Ideally, the exercises should be done by persons in classes or seminars or group meetings. Such organized settings allow better feedback, discussion, attention, and encouragement for responses to the exercises.

However you use this book, if you master the techniques in it, you will acquire a sense of satisfaction and accomplishment that comes only with knowing how to motivate others to do what they should do while they respond more positively to you.

What Is Systematic Attention and Approval?

With Young Children

Laura was a 4-year-old who wore a brace on her right leg. In the special preschool she attended, the teachers had tried and tried to coax her to use the playground climbing frame, to ride a tricycle, and to do other activities that her doctor and physical therapist had recommended in order to strengthen her muscles and improve her mobility. Unfortunately, Laura responded to their efforts by steadfastly refusing to join the other children in these activities. Then, as an experiment, the teachers began ignoring Laura unless she approached the climbing frame or a tricycle. If she did so they would exclaim, "Look at Laura. She's going to ride!" or "Look, Laura is starting to climb!" Within 3 days Laura was spending almost the entire outside play period riding a tricycle and climbing. A week later when her mother came to pick her up from preschool, Laura was perched atop the climbing frame and, to her mother's amazement, called out, "Look Mom, no hands!" Within weeks her physical therapist and doctor noted that her strength and mobility had markedly improved (from Hall, 1966).

At School

Robbie was a third-grade boy in an inner-city classroom. Although his teacher, Mrs. Bale, thought he was bright, he always received D's and F's on his report card and he was her most disruptive student. She frequently had to scold him for misbehavior and ask him to get back to work. It seemed he never studied. However, when Mrs. Bale began to notice when he was studying for as long as a minute or more, she went to his desk, said something to him about his work, or just put her hand on his shoulder, and Robbie started studying. Whenever she could, Mrs. Bale ignored Robbie when he was not studying. Much to her surprise, Robbie began studying harder. (By the end of the semester, he received a B in math and a C in spelling, the first grades above D since he entered school.) Soon it was easy for her to attend to him when he was working. He was no longer disruptive, and he became one of her hardest working students. Everyone who knew Robbie was amazed at the change (from Hall, Lund, & Jackson, 1968).

In Industry

A supervisor in a large Midwestern industrial plant was concerned because of the high number of electrical telephone components made by workers under his supervision that were rejected by quality control. He had faithfully carried out company procedure, which was to contact and reprimand workers whose part-rejection rate reached a certain percentage. In spite of this, the acceptance rate for a number of workers assigned to him barely met minimum and frequently dipped below. When he began giving systematic feedback to these workers when their work was above minimum standards, the rejection rate decreased dramatically. Workers who formerly had to be reprimanded began taking pride in almost 100% acceptance rate for parts they produced (Kempen, 1977).

These three incidents illustrate the use of systematic attention and approval to increase appropriate behavior. Adult attention in daily life is one key force in increasing and maintaining both desired and unwanted behavior in home, school, and work settings. Unfortunately, many persons squander their attention and approval in an unsystematic or haphazard way. Worse yet, some give nearly all their attention to unwanted behavior.

Systematic Attention Exercises

 EXERCISE 1:   Using Attention To Shift Location—The Pied Piper Effect

- This exercise may be carried out with one child or with several children.
- Observe children in a free-play situation (in the house, in the yard, or on the playground).
- Choose a particular area in the house (e.g., the living room), in the yard (e.g., at the swingset), or on the playground (e.g., a certain corner).

(continues)

- Try increasing the amount of time the children spend in that area by doing the following:

  1. Move to the area.

  2. If the children approach the area, speak to them.

  3. Make eye contact with the children in the area.

  4. Comment on whatever activity the children do in that area.

  5. Casually touch the children as you make comments (if appropriate to do so).

  6. If appropriate, participate in the activity with them.

  7. Ask questions about what they are doing.

Was there an increase in the amount of time the persons spent in the area you chose?   Yes ☐   No ☐

Were you surprised by the results?   Yes ☐   No ☐

Did it take long for you to increase time spent in the area you chose? Yes ☐   No ☐

To further observe how powerful your attention can be, try shifting the children to another area (room, section of the yard, playground) by moving to the area and paying attention to any who follow you there. How long did it take you to increase the number of children in the new area? _____ minutes?   _____ seconds?

EXERCISE 2:   Using Attention To Increase the Amount of Time a Person Spends Doing Something

Observe a child, a spouse, a friend, a coworker, your boss, or an employee who usually spends a limited amount of time practicing a music lesson, visiting with you, talking with you on the phone, stopping by your desk, or standing at the water cooler. Try increasing the amount of time they spend near you by doing one or more of the following:

1. Note the time.
2. Look at them (make eye contact).
3. Remain close to them while they are doing it.
4. Smile.
5. Comment on what they say.
6. Ask them to explain in more detail if they make a statement.
7. Ask them questions.
8. Make statements of approval about what they are doing.
9. Note the time.

(continues)

Describe whether or not you were able to increase the amount of time the persons spent in the activity.

_____

_____

_____

_____

How much longer than usual did the activity last? _____

_____

_____

Were you surprised by the results?   Yes ☐   No ☐

EXERCISE 3:   Using Attention and Approval on Someone New

- Select someone to whom you do not ordinarily have much to say. Say something approving, for example, to a waiter or waitress, someone from a different department where you work, a relative or neighbor, or one of your children's or spouse's friends.

- Practice using your attention (eye contact, questions, etc.) and approval (comments, head nods, and smiles) on that person the next time you see him or her.

Describe the results of this exercise.

Was the quality of your interaction different from usual?   Yes ☐   No ☐

If so, how? _____

_____

_____

_____

Practice

Having observed the effects of your attention on the behavior of others while carrying out these exercises, you should have a clear idea of what is meant by systematic attention and approval. It is simply the procedure of setting up a system to give attention and approval to increase a desired behavior. You are now ready to begin setting up a system to give attention and approval to increase a specific desired behavior in someone else. This begins by making certain you understand systematic attention and approval well enough to describe it.

In your own words, write (or tell) what **systematic attention and approval** is and what it does:

What it is: _____

_____

_____

_____

_____

What it does: _____

_____

_____

_____

_____

_____

You have the right idea if you said systematic attention and approval is noticing when someone is doing something desired and then giving him or her attention by commenting, looking at, touching, or expressing approval. The result is an increase in the desired behavior.

(continues)

Describe an incident that happened to you or that you observed in which attention or approval increased an appropriate behavior.

_____

_____

_____

_____

_____

Describe an event you experienced or observed in which you think someone could have or should have used attention and approval to increase a behavior.

_____

_____

_____

_____

_____

You might discuss your responses with a colleague or the professional working with you.

Using systematic attention and approval seems to be a very simple and commonsense approach. Nevertheless, it is sometimes difficult to begin using it without resorting to nags and reprimands. Many individuals have well-established habits that lead them to attempt to motivate people negatively. Even though a person may use attention and approval with certain persons in certain situations (e.g., friends when they come to dinner), he or she may rarely do the same with others in other situations (e.g., children at home or employees at work). Keep this in mind as you continue.

Basic Steps

Now that you know how systematic attention and approval affects the behavior of others, you are ready to learn the basic steps to increase a specific behavior in someone you know or with whom you work.

▶ Step 1: Define or pinpoint the behavior to change.

The first step is to define the behavior or behaviors you want to change. Because the procedure is designed to increase behavior, it is necessary to pinpoint a behavior or set of behaviors to be strengthened rather than negative behaviors to decrease. This is sometimes difficult because those behaviors that irritate or cause problems are usually more obvious than the behaviors you want to strengthen.

In some cases you can best see results of increasing a behavior you do want by looking for a decrease in a behavior you do not want. More of that later.

Another thing that makes definition difficult is that most people are not experienced at defining behavior. They frequently make statements such as, "Jaime never plays quietly," or "Alison never completes her work on time unless I get after her," or "Jim's work is always sloppy." When we look closely at a behavior, we usually find such statements are not true.

A good definition tells *who, what, when,* and *where*. Whose behavior is being pinpointed, exactly what is the behavior, and when and where does it take place?

Mrs. Harris was concerned because her 4-year-old son Jay never seemed to play by himself. As a result he was constantly underfoot and took a great deal of her time. This was especially troublesome when she was attempting to get dinner on the table. She had tried finding toys and activities for him in his room while she was fixing a meal, but invariably after a very short time he appeared in the kitchen, getting in her way, whining and crying, and generally interfering with meal preparation. She had tried scolding and spanking, but after a short interval Jay would be back in the kitchen fussing and getting in the way again.

When asked to define the behavior she wished to change, Mrs. Harris at first said she wanted to change Jay's coming in the kitchen and whining and asking for food while she was cooking. With help, however, Mrs. Harris began to pinpoint more specific behavior she wanted, which was for Jay to play quietly (i.e., quietly enough not to distract his mother) in his room, the family room, or in the backyard for 20 minutes or more at a time while she was preparing meals. She knew that to reach this minimum goal would be a vast improvement over her present situation.

Mrs. Harris selected a good definition because it told who, what, when, and where. Jay was *who*. Playing quietly enough not to distract his mother for 20 minutes was *what*. In his room, in the family room, or outdoors were *where*. While mother was fixing a meal was *when*.

Practice in Pinpointing

In the situation below, pinpoint an appropriate behavior that might be a target.

The floor supervisor is concerned because two of the salespersons in his department are slow to contact persons who enter the sales area to ask if they can be of assistance. He has seen customers turn and walk out of the department after waiting for the salespersons to finish a conversation with each other or to look up from other duties. He has reprimanded them on occasion but has noticed little improvement and that they avoid him whenever possible. He is reluctant to dismiss them because they are effective salespeople once they contact a customer and because his department already has a high turnover rate. He knows he must do something. Where should he begin?

Describe what behavior the supervisor should pinpoint and set out to change.

Who? _____

What? _____

When? _____

Where? _____

Did you focus on a specific behavior to be increased, for example, contacting customers within 1 minute after they enter the sales area even if it is merely to say, "I'll be with you in a minute"?   Yes ☐   No ☐

If you were able to check "yes," good! If you focused on an unwanted behavior, try again.

Did you answer the questions *who, what, when,* and *where?*   Yes ☐   No ☐

In defining your target, be sure to focus on behavior.

Using Labels

Sometimes people say they are concerned about "poor attitudes," "aggression," or "hostility." Unfortunately these descriptions are usually too negative and too general to pinpoint appropriate behavior. If at first you thought about using such a label, try instead to focus on a specific behavior you want to increase.

Describe how you would pinpoint a behavior you would like to change in your own child, your spouse, or someone you deal with in your work. (Try to choose a simple one you think you might have success with on your first try.)

Who? _____

What? _____

When? _____

Where? _____

Check your answer with the person working with you in this program. Did you describe a behavior you would like to increase?   Yes ☐   No ☐

If you both agree that the definition is a good one, make a check here ☐. If not, work on your definition until you can put a check in the box.

▶ Step 2: Measure the behavior.

The second step is to get a measure of the level of the behavior you want to change. This is important for two reasons:

1. It helps you understand later whether or not there really is a change in the behavior.

2. You may find that the behavior is not as much of a problem as you thought.

Sometimes when observing a behavior closely, you find that it changes in the direction you wanted it to go or that it is not really a problem. For example, the parents of one teenager were concerned with their son's arguing. When they began recording arguments, however, they found he argued about once every 2 weeks and it wasn't as bad a problem as they had thought (L. Cyrier, personal communication, April 1989). If this happens, so much the better. The thing to do then is to define another behavior to increase.

Remember to target a positive behavior. However, the easiest way to measure whether your approach is successful may be to measure a negative behavior. For example, although you may plan to increase nonfighting behavior, the easiest way to tell if you are successful is to see if the number of fights decreases.

Measuring Products of Behavior

There are several ways to measure a behavior. You can tell whether some behaviors have occurred by looking at the products they leave behind. A parent can tell whether a child did his or her chores by checking to see whether the trash is carried out, the bed is made, or the dishes are washed. An employer can check to see if a certain job is completed by looking at the product. A teacher can check a paper to see if a pupil has turned in correct answers on a math assignment.

In the following example, a parent kept track of whether a child picked up his or her room. The parent marked on the calendar the number of toys or items of clothing left out of place each day at bedtime.

Sun	Mon	Tues	Wed	Thurs	Fri	Sat
14	10	24	5	11	16	12

Counting Behaviors

Some behaviors are most easily measured by keeping a tally with paper and pencil each time a behavior occurs. Behaviors easily measured in this way include tantrums, arriving on time, saying thank you, and answering when spoken to.

In the following example, a teacher tallied the number of times a pupil remembered to raise her hand before speaking out in class during a daily discussion period.

Mon	Tues	Wed	Thurs	Fri
III	ℕ̵	II	ℕ̵ I	IIII

Measuring Whether or Not a Behavior Occurs in a Given Period

Sometimes it is easiest to notice whether or not a behavior occurs in a certain time period. For example, as shown in the following chart, one office worker kept track of whether or not her supervisor said something pleasant to her each morning and afternoon.

	Mon	Tues	Wed	Thurs	Fri	
A.M.	+	−	+	−	−	+ = yes
P.M.	−	−	−	−	+	− = no

Percentage of Behavior

Some behaviors can best be measured by the percentage of their occurrence. The number of opportunities may vary from time to time so the level can best be expressed in terms of the percentage of time the behavior occurred during periods of opportunity for occurrence.

For example, a parent may ask a child to do something 4 times one day, 6 times the next, and 5 times the next 2 days. The parent can keep track of how many times the child completes the task each day. If he or she responds appropriately 2 of 4 times the first day, 3 of 6 times the second, 4 out of 5 times the next, and 2 of 5 times the fourth, the percentage of behavior each day can be computed as shown in the following chart.

Day	Mon	Tues	Wed	Thurs
Record	2/4	3/6	4/5	2/5
Percent	50%	50%	80%	40%

If a mechanic properly fills out job cards at the garage where he works 1 in 7, 2 in 8, 3 in 10, 2 in 5, and 1 in 14 times during a 5-day week, the percentage of properly completed job cards can be recorded by his service manager as shown in the following chart.

Day	Mon	Tues	Wed	Thurs	Fri
Record	1/7	2/8	3/10	2/5	1/14
Percent	14%	25%	30%	40%	7%

Timing Behaviors

Some behaviors are best measured by how long they last or how long it takes someone to do something. For example, one parent recorded how many minutes his son spent doing homework each day, and another recorded how many hours and minutes it took her daughter to get dressed each day.

Using the following chart, an employer kept track of how much time an employee took to complete a certain task that was part of her daily responsibility.

Mon	Tues	Wed	Thurs	Fri
20 min	25 min	2 hrs, 3 min	28 min	58 min

For additional information on how to define and measure behavior, see Hall and Van Houten's (1983) book.

Selecting a Measurement Procedure

_____

Describe how you will measure the level of the behavior you plan to change. Remember, the purpose is to get an idea of the level of the behavior *before* you try to change it.

_____

_____

_____

_____

_____

_____

_____

_____

Recording the Behavior

Although you may be keeping a tally of the behavior you have selected to measure on a piece of paper, a calendar, or somewhere else, also make a permanent record, such as the following chart.

Day or Session	1	2	3	4	5	6	7	8
Level of Behavior								

When you have enough information about the behavior, define what you think is the average level of the behavior.

On the average, the behavior occurs about _____

_____

_____

Graphing the Behavior

This is an optional activity to obtain a visual picture of the level of a behavior by putting it on a graph. For example, the mother who counted the number of toys and items of clothing left out of place at bedtime in a previous example made the following graph.

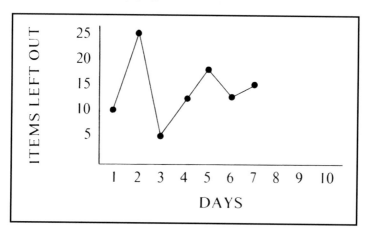

The office worker made this graph of whether or not her supervisor said something pleasant to her.

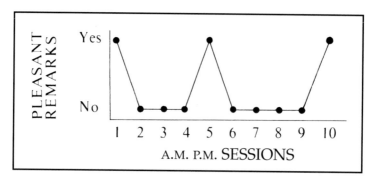

Charting Behavior Exercise (optional)

At the end of this text, before the References, is a sample Raw Data Sheet that many persons use to create a visual display of the target behavior. You may want to use that form to display the behavior you have chosen to change. The vertical axis shows the level of the behavior. Days or sessions go across the horizontal axis.

Chart the behavior you have measured by using a data point for each observation session. This record of the behavior before you try to change it is called a *baseline*. Ask your instructor to help you chart it if you are uncertain about how to do it. (Further discussion of measuring and charting behavior may be found in Hall & Van Houten, 1983.)

▶ **Step 3: Set a goal for the target behavior.**

Once you have measured the level of the behavior you wish to change, it is a good idea to set a goal. For example, the mother who found that her child always left out 14 or 15 toys each night decided that if she could change that to 3 it would be an acceptable level. The office worker decided that it would be a marked improvement if her supervisor said something positive to her at least every other day.

Define the target level of the behavior you have chosen. _____

_____

_____

_____

_____

_____

_____

▶ **Step 4: Select the kind of attention and approval to use.**

Once the behavior you want to increase is defined, and you are measuring it to get a good idea of its present level and to help you decide how much you want to change it, you should select the kind of attention and approval you will use. You should keep several things in mind:

1. What works with one person may not work with another.

2. Varying the attention and approval you give and pairing it with other good things will make your efforts more effective.

3. Specific praise is usually more effective than general praise or attention.

Put Variety in Your Reinforcement

Comments such as, "Good boy, you got it right that time!" are more likely to motivate a 4-year-old than a 40-year-old. The same comment may or may not work with a 14-year-old. With young children, touching, a pat on the head, or a squeeze as they work or play is a good way to provide attention. This is especially true if they are engaged in appropriate behavior you wish to increase but not interrupt.

While such contact can be very acceptable with one of your children or your spouse, it could backfire if used with an employee, your boss, or others who might misinterpret your touching. Some might even charge you with sexual harassment.

The words and phrases you use to give attention and approval should be varied from person to person. Occasionally, someone will use the same word or phrase over and over until it gets boring or even irritating. Be careful not to overuse phrases such as "Very good!" or "Good girl!" Varying your approving comments will reflect your sincerity in giving them. One way to find good words to use is to listen to a person and his or her peers and try the words and phrases they use to express approval among themselves. The following words and phrases are ones you may want to consider trying out on different audiences.

Cool, man!	You amaze me!
Fantastic!	Let's see that again!
All right!	I don't see how you do it!
Way to go!	Sweet!
Give me five.	I never would have thought of that.
Beautiful!	You're number one!
You're neat.	What a shot (picture, speech, idea)!
That's a winner!	Wow!
That is really exciting!	Very perceptive question!
An excellent point!	Awesome!

Public or Private Praise—Which To Use?

When Jerry's boss praised him during sales meetings, Jerry turned red and became uncomfortable. Before long his boss learned to speak to him privately, take him to lunch, or write him a letter of commendation. From then on, Jerry always responded positively.

Persons such as Jerry find public acclaim to be anything but positive. Others will do almost anything to be in the limelight.

Ask yourself what kind of attention will work best with the person you are trying to change. Check below which kind of attention you think will work best.
- ☐ Public attention and approval?
- ☐ Private attention and approval?
- ☐ Both?

Using Specific Praise

In addition to remembering that your attention and approval must be appropriate, it is important to be specific about the behavior of concern (Bernhardt & Forehand, 1975).

If you wish to attend to a child who is playing with a friend rather than fighting, it is better to say, "My, you two are playing so well together and having such fun!" than to say, "Darien, you're a good girl."

A note to a secretary saying, "Lorretta, you got that report out in record time, thank you," is better than, "You're a good secretary."

"Steve, I want to give you credit for coming up with that idea about the Purdy account—I'd never have thought of it," will be more effective than, "Steve, thank you for your efforts on the Purdy account."

Strengthening Praise and Approval by Pairing Them with Other Good Things

On several occasions Aletha overhears her mother telling her grandmother on the phone or a neighbor in the yard how much help Aletha is with her baby sister. On such occasions Aletha beams. Aletha does not hesitate the next time her mother asks her to bring a diaper or to hold the baby.

When the district manager came around, Clyde asked his top salesperson, Jeremy, to go along to lunch and to share with the manager a new sales technique he was using. Jeremy continued his record pace in selling and turned down another job offer because, as he told his wife, "Clyde really appreciates me and backs me up. I'm not sure I'd get that kind of treatment at a bigger company."

Holly praised her second-grade students for working quietly and finishing their work on time. She also let them use the last 5 minutes of the class period to play a favorite game. Two or three times a month, she would say to her class, "I just can't believe what good workers you are! Because everyone did such a nice job on this week's spelling (or writing, or math), we will celebrate by going out to the playground for an extra recess."

Debra thanks her teenage daughter, Meghann, for fixing dinner three times each week and for running errands in the car. But fairly frequently she asks Meghann at the same time she is thanking her if she wants to use the car that weekend or if she needs gas money. Meghann and her mother have a good relationship.

In each of the above situations, someone gave substance to attention and approval by backing it up with other actions. Praise is much more likely to maintain its effectiveness if it is accompanied by action showing that the person giving it really means what he or she says.

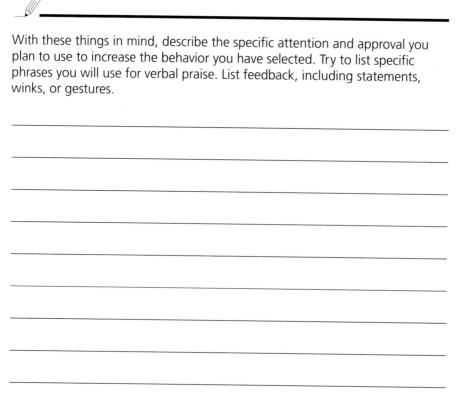

With these things in mind, describe the specific attention and approval you plan to use to increase the behavior you have selected. Try to list specific phrases you will use for verbal praise. List feedback, including statements, winks, or gestures.

_____

_____

_____

_____

_____

_____

_____

(continues)

Do you plan to pair your attention with any other good things? If your answer is yes, tell what privilege or activity you plan to include.

_____

_____

_____

▶ **Step 5: Determine when and how often.**

In School

Noelle had a history of getting into squabbles with her fourth-grade classmates. Her teacher, Ms. Beasley, decided to help her overcome this problem. On Monday Ms. Beasley talked to Noelle and told her she knew that Noelle could get along better with her classmates. Noelle agreed and promised to try very hard not to quarrel or fight. The teacher, who had been keeping a record, was delighted to notice that by Friday noon Noelle had avoided any squabbles since their talk on Monday. She decided to praise Noelle as soon as school was dismissed for the day. During the last period on Friday, however, Noelle had a shouting match with a boy who had a habit of teasing her. Ms. Beasley talked to Noelle when school was dismissed. She said she was really proud of her for going all week without a squabble even though she had gotten into one right at the very end of the day. Ms. Beasley was disappointed that Noelle had three more fights the next week. She decided praise and attention did not work. What mistake did Ms. Beasley make?

At Home

Doug was enjoying the evening paper after a hard day at the office. He noticed that, for a change, his son, Brendon, was playing quietly rather than whining or crying or asking him to play a game. He thought about giving Brendon a few seconds of his attention by commenting about how quietly he was playing and then decided, "No, I'd better not interrupt him while he's being so quiet." Within 2 minutes Brendon was fussing and his father found himself scolding his son for bothering him. There was no more peace and quiet before dinner that day. What should Doug have done?

In Business

A Midwestern businessman advertised to hire workers at three times the salary being offered by other companies. Although several hundred persons answered the ad, not one accepted the offer. At the interviews, the business-man proposed to pay potential employees only one half the going rate for the next 5 years. The rest he would invest in the business. With this increased cap-ital he would build up the business, and after 5 years he would pay them for those 5 years at three times the salary they would get if he had to pay them a regular salary immediately. Is it surprising no one took the job?

These situations show that:

1. To be truly effective, attention and approval as well as other rein-forcers must come during or immediately following the behavior to be increased.

2. One must be careful not to give attention following *unwanted* behav-ior, for that unwanted behavior is the one likely to increase.

3. Even powerful incentives such as money are ineffective if they come too long after the behavior.

4. It is extremely important to provide attention and approval while a behavior is occurring or immediately after it happens.

Make a list of some kinds of systematic attention and approval you can give during and after desired behavior occurs.

Things I can do while the behavior is occurring: _____

_____

_____

_____

_____

_____

_____

_____

_____

(continues)

Things I can do right after the behavior: _____

_____

_____

_____

_____

_____

_____

Under certain circumstances it may be difficult or disruptive to give attention during behavior. In such cases list only what you will do right after the behavior.

What To Do If You Have Little or No Behavior with Which To Work

Some persons find it difficult to give attention or to show approval to a behavior because there is so little of it. Quite often a parent will say, "But how can I show approval when he remembers to do only one or two chores each week and he should be doing them every day?" Or, "He fusses and cries so much that there is not a day when I could praise him for being good." An employer may say, "But why should I show approval for her to be here on time? That's part of her job."

In each case it may be difficult at first to see how or why the person should be given attention and approval. Nevertheless, in each case, what has been tried in the past, which probably includes reminders and reprimands when the person does not perform, has not worked. Therefore, it may be worthwhile to try something new rather than using ineffective procedures over and over. Unfortunately many people resist using positive procedures even when they seek help because the negative procedures they have tried have failed.

When there is very little positive behavior, there are two alternatives. One is to watch carefully and, when the behavior occurs even at a low level, begin giving systematic attention and approval. Sometimes the results are amazing. For one thing, when you begin looking for the behavior you want rather than focusing on the behavior you do not want, you may be surprised at how much good behavior there is.

Mr. Delquadri took a parenting course but he was skeptical about whether attention and approval would work with his son, Joe. Joe was just plain lazy. It seemed Joe never did his chores or helped at home unless his father or mother reminded him to do so. Even then he did them reluctantly. The parenting leader urged him to try praising Joe if he did do anything on his own. Though skeptical, Mr. Delquadri began looking for behavior he could praise. He found that in the next 2 days Joe mowed the lawn and washed the car without reminding. Although he did not carry out the trash, his room was a mess, and he violently objected to having to take his younger brother to get a haircut, Mr. Delquadri did comment about how nice the lawn looked and thanked him for washing the car. He even asked Joe if he wanted to go to an empty parking lot to practice driving since he would be taking driver's training the next fall. Mr. Delquadri was surprised at the results. Not only did Joe respond far more positively than expected, but his father also enjoyed the driving lesson. The next day, to his surprise, Joe carried out the trash and then beamed when his father said, "Son, you really seem to be accepting responsibility. That's a big help to your mom."

The following week Joe again mowed the lawn without being told, cleaned the car inside and out, and remembered to carry out the trash. His room was still a mess but Mr. Delquadri was pleased at the improvement in Joe's behavior and also at how much his relationship with his son had improved.

You may feel, like Mr. Delquadri, that your son or daughter, employee, or student does so little that is worth praising that there is no place to start. If that is so, you may need to lower your standards. In the beginning you may have to give praise and attention for a little of what you want in order to begin moving someone in the right direction toward the larger goal. In technical terms this is called behavior shaping.

Prompting Desired Behavior

Julie had a new baby. With two boys, ages 3½ and 6, she had her hands full. In an effort to make things easier, she decided to get Spencer, her 3½-year-old, to help keep his room clean. She decided to start by praising him the first time he put away his toys, books, and clothes either on his own or when she told him to do so. Unfortunately, she found that, even when she told him to clean up his room, he would usually leave some toys lying around or would shove some under the bed. Julie found articles of clothing on the bed or in a chair, and books in the toy box or on the floor rather than in the bookcase where they belonged.

After waiting 5 days in the hope he would clean his room well enough that she would not have to go in and pick up after him, she realized that it might be weeks or months before he did a praiseworthy job. Therefore, she decided to prompt the behavior she wanted by saying, "Come on Spencer, let's go clean up your room." She then said, "First let's pick up the toys. I see toys on the floor and the bed, and I even think I see one under the bed. Let's put them in the toy box where they belong." As Spencer helped pick up the toys, she made a number of comments on what a good job he was doing and how nice his room was beginning to look. Then she said, "You're a good boy, Spencer, you've picked up all the toys. Now let's see if there are any books that aren't in the bookcase." Spencer found one on a chair and put it in the bookcase. His mother again praised him and then said, "I see another one here in your toy box; can you find it?" Spencer promptly did and was given a hug and praise for putting it in the bookcase. Then Julie turned her attention to the clothes, helping Spencer put his shoes in the closet and a dirty shirt and underwear in the clothes hamper. Then she took his hand, stood in the middle of the room, and said, "Look Spencer, you cleaned your room! How nice it looks, your toys are in the toy box, your books are in the bookcase, your shoes are in the closet, and your dirty clothes are in the hamper. You're such a big help. You cleaned your room!"

At supper she told her husband how well Spencer had cleaned his room. The next day she repeated the procedure. The third day she asked him to do the toys all by himself—making a big deal out of it. Within a week Spencer was consistently putting his toys, books, and clothes away without any attention other than being asked to clean up his room and being told what a good job he had done.

Taking time to tell or demonstrate what is meant by doing a good job is often a necessary step. If your children are not doing a good job, it may be they do not know what you expect. If this is the case, prompt or show them how to do it and immediately show approval, even if you have to help them.

Check to see whether you think the person whose behavior you want to change does at least some of what you want. Is there enough behavior there that you can give systematic attention and approval to those low levels until they increase?   Yes ☐   No ☐   I'll have to observe a while longer to see ☐.

Check whether you think you may have to tell or show the person whose behavior you'd like to change just what is expected in order for you to give attention and approval.   No I don't think it will be necessary ☐.
Yes I think I will have to ☐.

If yes, describe what you will do to prompt the appropriate behavior.

_____

_____

_____

(continues)

Will you show attention and approval when the behavior occurs, even if you have to prompt it?   Yes ☐   No ☐

How soon will you be able to withdraw your prompts? _____

_____

Will you need to continue your attention and approval even after the new behavior is established?   Yes ☐   No ☐

▶ **Step 6: Review.**

You are now ready to use your attention and approval in a systematic way to increase a behavior you have selected. In order to review exactly what you will do, summarize the information from the first five steps below:

1. Define or pinpoint the behavior.

Describe the behavior you will change.

Who? _____

What? _____

When? _____

Where? _____

2. Measure the behavior.

Describe the current level of the behavior you have measured. _____

_____

_____

3. Set a goal for the target behavior.

Describe the level of behavior you would like to establish. _____

_____

_____

(continues)

4. Select the kind of attention and approval to use.

Describe the attention and approval you are going to use. _____

_____

_____

Will you pair your attention and approval with any other activity to make it more powerful?　　Yes ☐　No ☐

If yes, what activity? _____

_____

5. Determine when and how often to use attention and approval.

Describe when you plan to provide attention and approval. _____

_____

_____

Will you plan to attend to small amounts of the desired behavior at first?
Yes ☐　No ☐

Will you use a prompting procedure to help get the behavior started?
Yes ☐　No ☐

▶ **Step 7: Practice by role-playing systematic attention and approval.**

For persons to be more sure of themselves as they begin to use systematic attention and approval, it helps to rehearse what they are going to do. A good role-playing procedure involves three persons. Two persons act out the role-playing situation while the third person records what happens. Then the three persons switch positions and go through the scene again, then switch once more so that each has a chance to play the roles of the person giving attention, the person receiving it, and the person acting as recorder.

In the following scene, three teachers role-played the use of systematic attention and approval. Mr. Greenwood was assigned the role of a sixth-grade student named Charlie, Ms. Terry the role of the teacher, and Ms. Carta the role of recorder.

CHARLIE:　　It is a math study period. You have been goofing off trying to attract the attention of the teacher and your neighbors without too much success. Finally, in desperation you get out your paper and begin working.

TEACHER: You have been in the habit of getting after Charlie and reminding him to go to work, usually from the vantage point of being seated at your desk. However, you have decided to catch him working and to begin using specific praise to increase working behavior.

RECORDER: You will observe the teacher, mark the recording sheet, and check the points the teacher remembers to include in using systematic attention and approval.

The teachers prepared a role-playing recording sheet that was to be checked by all three teachers. First, Ms. Carta checked it as Ms. Terry played the teacher. Then Ms. Terry checked Mr. Greenwood as he took the teacher's role, and then Mr. Greenwood provided feedback as Ms. Carta played the teacher.

Sample Recording Sheet: Role-Playing

Teacher Behavior (Attention and Approval)	Person Playing Teacher		
	Ms. Terry	**Mr. Greenwood**	**Ms. Carta**
1. Look at student	✔	✔	✔
2. Move within 3 feet of student	✔	✔	✔
3. Make specific comment on work	✔	✔	✔
4. Smile	0	✔	✔
5. Reinforce him while he is working	✔	✔	✔
6. Touch student (optional)	0	0	✔

The sheet indicates that Ms. Terry did not smile or touch Charlie; Mr. Greenwood met all the criteria but did not touch Charlie, an optional way of providing attention; and Ms. Carta achieved all five criteria for providing systematic attention and approval in this situation.

In the case of Charlie, the teacher planned in advance the specific things to do.

On the recording sheet that follows, list in the numbered column the ways you plan to carry out your systematic attention and approval program. You probably should look at the person, move within 3 feet, make specific comments, smile, and do so during or within 5 seconds of the occurrence of the behavior. Check with your instructor. If he or she agrees with your list, put a check here ☐.

Your instructor, your spouse, or another person should help you set up a role-playing situation to practice before you begin. In doing so, one should play the person whose behavior is to be increased, one the person giving attention, and one the recorder. Each should shift roles so that you go through the exercise three times, once for each position.

Set the scene describing the following roles:

Target person: _____

_____

_____

_____

_____

Attention giver: _____

_____

_____

_____

_____

Recorder: Will guide the role-playing and give feedback.

(continues)

Recording Sheet: Role-Playing

Teacher Behavior (Attention and Approval)	Person Playing Teacher		
	1	2	3
1.			
2.			
3.			
4.			
5.			
6.			

▶ **Step 8: Maintain behavior.**

To increase Robbie's study behavior, Mrs. Bale initially began giving him attention each time he studied for a minute. As he began studying more and more, however, she found she needed to give him attention less and less frequently. In fact, after a time she maintained his good study behavior with less attention than she had had to give to his former disruptive behavior (from Hall, Lund, & Jackson, 1968).

Even though at first it is best to give frequent attention and approval to the behavior you want to increase, as soon as it is established, it can be maintained by less frequent attention. A parent can increase the amount of time a child will practice music lessons by herself by sitting with her and frequently commenting on her playing. After a time the parent can leave the child alone before returning to attend to and encourage her playing. By gradually increasing the intervals of being gone from 2 minutes, to 4 minutes, and so on, before long the child will play longer and longer without attention, and it is easier for the parent to maintain the behaviors when the intervals between attention are longer.

In the same way, an employer can increase the performance of a worker by giving daily feedback about good performance. Later, less and less frequent feedback (perhaps on a weekly and then even monthly basis) will be the most effective way to maintain the improved behavior.

Remember, however, not to decrease attention and approval too quickly or the behavior may begin to decrease. If that happens it will be necessary to increase the amount of attention and approval and begin decreasing it again at a slower pace.

_____

Describe the best way to maintain behavior once it is established at higher levels.

_____

_____

_____

_____

Does this mean you should stop using attention and approval completely?
Yes ☐   No ☐

If you said that to maintain behavior efficiently it should be given attention less frequently, you are correct. Of course, you will need to keep giving some attention and approval or the behavior will probably stop. No one will continue a task indefinitely without some form of reinforcement (see *How To Maintain Behavior,* Esveldt-Dawson & Kazdin, 1998).

▶ **Step 9: Be aware of potential problems.**

Unwanted Behavior May Increase at First

Negative behaviors sometimes show an increase before they begin to decrease. This is especially true if, in the past, the negative behavior has received much attention (even in the form of scolding or reprimands) and you are now giving attention only to appropriate behavior. You must be prepared for an increase of unwanted behavior that has been getting attention before the behavior you are trying to increase takes over. This is one reason to continue to keep a record of the behavior. Most of the time you will see an increase in the behavior you comment on, praise, and show approval to in other ways. If, however, this does not happen, do not give up. In most cases, the negative behavior will soon decrease and the desired behavior will increase as expected.

Describe what may happen when you first begin using systematic attention and approval.

_____

_____

_____

_____

_____

What should you do if this does happen? _____

_____

_____

_____

_____

If you said that negative behavior may increase at first but you should keep on attending to appropriate behavior until it increases, you are correct.

Some Persons May Reject Your Attention and Approval

Some persons will at first reject praise statements or attention to appropriate behavior. For example, one student tore up his paper when his teacher commented on what a good job he had done. This happened the next time she praised him as well. Rather than getting upset, she waited until his next paper and commented again. He looked at her, started to reach for the paper, then smiled and said, "Yeah, I guess it is pretty good." From then on his work improved daily.

Teenagers may make comments such as, "Don't use that on me" or "I don't care what you think." This is especially true if you have been in the habit of giving reprimands. Nevertheless, if you keep calm and respond quietly and positively, saying, for example, "I can see that, but I still appreciated what you did," chances are the behavior you want will increase.

Keep in mind that you do not want to be controlled by what the person *says*. Observe what the person *does*. If the behavior you want increases, then you know that your attention and approval system is working, no matter what the person says.

On the other hand, it is a good idea to take a look at the kind of attention you are providing to consider whether another form of attention and approval might be more effective.

Describe what you should do if at first the person rejects your attention and approval.

_____

_____

_____

_____

_____

_____

You are correct if you said that you should not act upset and you should look at the results rather than what the person says. Take a look at the attention you are giving to make sure it is right for that person.

Another reminder is not to wait too long before giving attention and approval. If you wait too long, you may find yourself attending to negative behavior. Remember to catch the person being good before he or she has a chance to spoil your program.

▶ **Step 10: Evaluate the results.**

Once you begin your attempt to change a behavior, it is important to continue observing the behavior you measured to see if there is a change in the level. Be prepared to record the results of your efforts on a simple form like the following:

Days or Sessions	1	2	3	4	5	6	7	8	9
Level of Behavior									

How does this level compare with the average level before you began?

An increase ☐   A decrease ☐   No change ☐

How did the person seem to respond? _____

_____

_____

_____

Was there an initial increase in the undesired behavior?   Yes ☐   No ☐

When did you first notice an increase in the desired behavior? _____

_____

_____

_____

Have you had to vary or change the attention and approval you are providing?
Yes ☐   No ☐

If so, how have you changed it? _____

_____

_____

_____

Have you met the change goal you set on page 24?   Yes ☐   No ☐

(continues)

Do you think the behavior is well enough established for you to shift to giving less attention and approval?   Yes ☐   No ☐

Do you have a new behavior you are ready to try to change using attention and approval?   Yes ☐   No ☐

If yes, what is it?

Who? _____

_____

What? _____

_____

When? _____

_____

Where? _____

_____

Making a graph of a behavior provides a visual picture of how the behavior has been affected. The following graph shows the effects of a mother's attention to the number of toys and clothing items left out by her son.

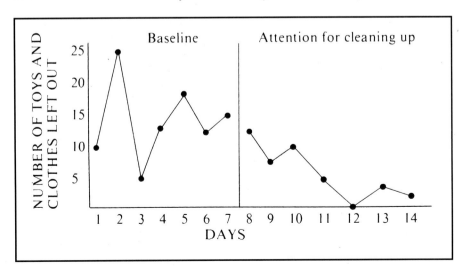

Charting Behavior (optional)

On the Raw Data Sheet provided at the end of this manual, make a record of the behavior you are changing through systematic attention and approval. If you have already charted the level of behavior before you tried to change it (baseline), draw a vertical line to show where the baseline record ends, as was done in the example. Now chart the behavior to show the level on each day or session after you began trying to change it. This will give you a visual comparison and it will be easy to see how much the behavior has changed. Ask your instructor if you need help in charting.

Where To From Here?

This book has explained how to use systematic attention and approval to motivate other persons and, at the same time, to improve the quality of your interactions with them. The examples used were simple and straightforward and come from real-life situations. They were chosen to be representative of a variety of behaviors that can be managed with systematic attention and approval. The list of behaviors that can be changed using these techniques is almost unlimited; however, some behaviors cannot be handled with systematic attention and approval alone. Physical problems that interfere with motor movements or the acquisition of certain skills obviously cannot be overcome with the application of approval and attention alone, but even problems of that kind can be improved by using systematic attention and approval in conjunction with other treatment procedures.

This book has helped you learn to be a better motivator. What you have learned is how to develop your own natural skills and how to dispense your own praise and attention in ways that motivate other persons in a positive way. How skilled you become at using systematic attention and approval is limited only by the amount of effort you want to put into it, and by the amount of reinforcement (attention and approval) you get from others in your efforts to change behavior in them and in yourself. The principles you have learned are the same no matter how far you go in developing your skills of approval and attention. As you use the principles you have learned, they become more and more natural and more and more a part of your own personality and the image you project to other persons. In other words, if you become skilled at providing others with pleasant consequences in the form of encouragement and approval, people, including family members, will like you better than if you try to motivate them by scolding or reprimands.

Putting It All Together

This section should be reviewed and filled out 2 weeks or more after you have initiated your behavior change program. It will provide feedback to your instructor on how well it worked for you.

1. Was your first attempt successful?   Yes ☐   No ☐

2. What changes in behavior did you observe? _____

_____

_____

3. What problems did you encounter? _____

_____

_____

4. Were you able to solve these problems? If so, how? _____

_____

_____

5. Describe briefly any other behaviors you have changed. _____

_____

_____

6. Do you plan to continue?   Yes ☐   No ☐   With whom? _____

_____

_____

7. Is systematic attention and approval a skill you can now use effectively?
   Yes ☐   No ☐   Maybe ☐

(continues)

8. Comments: _____

_____

_____

_____

_____

_____

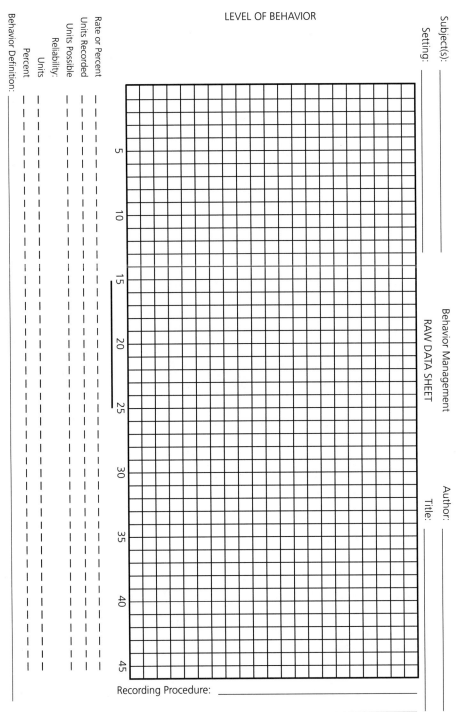

Subject(s): _____

Setting: _____

Behavior Management

RAW DATA SHEET

Author: _____

Title: _____

LEVEL OF BEHAVIOR

Rate or Percent | — | — |
Units Recorded | — | — |
Units Possible | — | — |
Reliability: | — | — |
Units | — | — |
Percent | — | — |
Behavior Definition: _____

Recording Procedure: _____

References

Allen, K. E., Hart, B. M., Buell, J. S., Harris, F. R., & Wolf, M. M. (1964). Effects of social reinforcement on isolate behavior of a nursery school child. *Child Development, 35,* 511–518.

Axelrod, S. (1983). *Behavior modification for the classroom teacher.* New York: McGraw-Hill.

Axelrod, S., Hall, R. V., & Maxwell, A. (1972). Use of peer attention to increase appropriate classroom behavior. *Behavior Therapy, 3,* 349–351.

Bernhardt, A. J., & Forehand, R. (1975). The effects of labeled and unlabeled praise upon lower and middle class children. *Journal of Experimental Child Psychology, 19,* 536–543.

Brown, R., Copeland, R., & Hall, R. V. (1972). The school principal as a behavior modifier. *Journal of Educational Research, 4,* 175–180.

Cossairt, A., Hall, R. V., & Hopkins, B. L. (1973). The effects of experimenter's instructions, feedback and praise on teacher praise and student attending behavior. *Journal of Applied Behavior Analysis, 6,* 89–100.

Daniels, A. C. (1994). *Bringing out the best in people: How to apply the astonishing power of positive reinforcement.* New York: McGraw-Hill.

Esveldt-Dawson, K., & Kazdin, A. E., (1998). *How to maintain behavior.* Austin, TX: PRO-ED.

Hall, R. V., & Broden, M. (1967). Behavior changes in brain-injured children through social reinforcement. *Journal of Experimental Child Psychology, 5,* 463–479.

Hall, R. V., Lund, D., & Jackson, D. (1968). Effects of teacher attention on study behavior. *Journal of Applied Behavior Analysis, 1,* 1–12.

Hall, R. V., Panyan, M., Rabon, D., & Broden, M. Instructing beginning teachers in reinforcement procedures which improve classroom control. *Journal of Applied Behavior Analysis, 1,* 315–322.

Harris, F. R., Wolf, M. M., & Baer, D. M. (1964). Effects of adult social reinforcement on child behavior. *Young Children, 20,* 8–17.

Hart, B. M., Allen, K. E., Buell, J. S., Harris, F. R., & Wolf, M. M. (1964). Effects of social reinforcement on operant crying. *Journal of Experimental Child Psychology, 1,* 145–153.

Kazdin, A. E. (1994). *Behavior modification in applied settings.* Pacific Grove, CA: Brooks/Cole.

Kempen, R. W. (1977). *The effects of performance standards, feedback and contingent supervisor praise on the performance of industrial workers.* Unpublished masters thesis.

Kempen, R. W., & Hall, R. V. (1977). Reduction of industrial absenteeism: results of a behavioral approach. *Journal of Organizational Behavior Management, 1,* 1–21.

Kirby, F. D., & Shields, F. (1972). Modification of arithmetic response rate and attending behavior in a seventh-grade student. *Journal of Applied Behavior Analysis, 5,* 79–84.

Sulzer-Azeroff, B., & Mayer, G. R. (1991). *Behavior analysis for lasting change.* Fort Worth, TX: Holt, Rinehart and Winston.

Notes

Notes

Notes